To I

D1624239

*Reflections on the
Promise and Law*

To Do My Best

*Reflections on the
Promise and Law*

THE GUIDE
ASSOCIATION

Published by The Guide Association
17–19 Buckingham Palace Road
London SW1W 0PT
© The Guide Association 1996
Reprinted 1996, 1997

Compiled by The Law Resources Writing Group:
Elizabeth Anderson, Catherine Bartlett, Jane Lewes,
Sue Moore, Lindsay Sanderson and Sue Wales

Edited by: Alice Forbes and Anne Mable

Designed by: Catherine Summers

Cover illustration by: Anna Hancock

Printed in England by: The Cromwell Press,
Melksham

The Guide Association's Trading Service ordering code:
66019

ISBN 0 85260 140 9

Readers are reminded that during the life span of this
publication, policy changes may be made by The Guide
Association which will affect the accuracy of information
contained within these pages.

Preface

This book is meant for Guiders when they are teaching the Law and Promise and for all who wish to reflect on their understanding of the Promise and Law.

Years ago when I was going to make my Ranger Promise, we were asked "Do you know what your honour means?" and we were to reply: "My honour means that I can be trusted".

Well, up to that moment I'd never really given it much thought, but when it was put to me, it made me stop and think.

So my point is that it is always worth explaining words properly. Especially difficult ones, like Honesty, Reliability, Trustworthiness, core words for Guiding and those on which it was founded.

This book is full of similar personal impressions which will help you to understand the Promise and Law.

Margaret

Her Royal Highness The Princess Margaret,
Countess of Snowdon
President

Foreword

Many Guiders have asked for a book 'to help them with the Promise'. As the bulk of this book has been written by those very Guiders, it should be seen as a recognition of the accumulated wisdom and experience of our Guiders and an affirmation of their value as leaders of our girls and young women.

During recent consultations about the Promise and Law, thousands of letters were received expressing the centrality of the Promise in people's lives, both within and outside the Movement. The thoughts expressed in those letters reflected the quality of leadership we have in The Guide Association and this is one way of demonstrating that every Guider has a contribution to make to our developing understanding of the Promise.

As the recent reviews of the Promise and Law were conducted separately, they are frequently referred to as distinct from each other. We should like to emphasise that the Law is an intrinsic part of the Promise and as such, any reference to the Promise implies reference to the Law.

The initial ideas for the book were taken from letters written during the Promise debate and they were expanded by various people with wide experience in Guiding. We are particularly grateful to our President for graciously writing the Preface and our thanks go to all who so willingly contributed and who responded to the Promise and Law consultations.

The small team which has worked on this book hopes that it answers the need for a resource on the Promise. They have been ably helped by staff at Commonwealth Headquarters and appreciation for their work can best be shown by using the book in every way possible: for personal reflections, for group discussion, for trainings, for Commissioners' 'instant offerings', for Guide's Own, and by letting us know how it is being used.

Catherine Bartlett

Catherine Bartlett
Chairman
The Law Resources Writing Group
September 1996

> *Promising to 'do one's best' in whatever*
> *one is doing, whether Guide or non-Guide,*
> *is surely a firm foundation*
> *on which to build one's life.*

Every building has to be based on a firm foundation otherwise it will topple in the first storm. Equally, each of us will be able to withstand whatever life throws at us if we 'do our best'. This is not purely a code for our Guiding activities but applies to every aspect of our lives. It also suggests a developing maturity.

Whilst a seven-year-old may interpret 'doing her best' as not fighting with her brother, as she grows into an adult 'doing her best' may involve campaigning against human injustice. She is growing stronger just as the building grows stronger, brick by brick.

If I always "do my best", no one can ask for more.

A promise is not a password to get us into Guides.

When do you use passwords? Do you remember them from childhood games? Do you use them to gain access to a computer or classified information? Do you use them to pass through a security net?

Passwords are intended to keep people out. They are a means of ensuring that only the right people are allowed in and those who cannot give the right word are denied access. Passwords are about excluding.

Guiding is for all, and the Promise, the cornerstone of our Movement, is for all who can understand and accept it. It is not a quick-fix solution for entry that is open only to those who can recite the words and can understand their meaning. It is for all who struggle to understand and try to live out its meaning.

Live and grow with the Promise.

No one at the age of 11 knows all about God.
It takes a lifetime and one is still learning.
Like a lot of other things.

Knowing all about God is surely an impossibility. It is the process of searching and seeking which is so important, whatever the age of the person.

What needs to be stressed to the child or adult renewing or making her Promise is that, in the presence of witnesses, she is making a commitment to learn more about her faith (or lack of it!).

There is no particular starting point, it depends on each individual; and there is certainly no finish!

I may not know all about God
but God knows all about me.

Guiding belongs to the girls of today. Let's keep it simple for them so they can have fun living by a code they can understand.

At its most simple, Guiding is a magic game with a serious purpose. It aims to offer girls and young women the chance to learn some of life's significant lessons – lessons that maybe they won't learn anywhere else. The magic comes with the Method – the balance of the Five Essential Elements (individuals, groups, democracy, variety and values) combining to provide real learning which the girl can transfer to the whole of her life.

It is a game designed to be played by the young – voluntarily, simply and informally. Too often we, the adults, make Guiding too complicated for the girls; this robs them of the chance to play *their* game as they want to.

Like all the best games, Guiding should be simple enough to be played by everyone.

Having doubts about beliefs and questioning familiar habits is healthy and can lead to more thoughtful attitudes and appreciation of values.

If you are absolutely certain about all that you do and believe, then you are not open to new views and can become dogmatic.

When working with Rainbows we can tell them what is right and what is wrong and they will accept this. For example, we can make it quite plain that it is wrong to tell lies or to steal.

But as girls get older, we want them to be able to think for themselves and be responsible: they therefore have to question ideas which are put before them.

Members of the Senior Section can debate whether there are extreme times when one might have to steal in order, for example, to save someone else's life.

Such discussion, questioning traditional values, helps us to have a better understanding of our beliefs and to develop as whole people.

Our understanding of the Promise will develop through questioning and debate.

Trusty, loyal, helpful, sisterly,
courteous, kind, obedient, smiling, thrifty,
pure in thought and mind.
An excellent guidance for life.

These words may not be instantly familiar to the young today but their spirit still lives on.

Ask a Guide what the Guide Law means to her and she will tell you it means looking after the environment, not being nasty to her little brother, helping with the housework, doing her homework or maybe doing something for her community or the less fortunate at home and overseas.

Although the words are important, it is their meaning that must shine through. They must give each girl ideals to strive for which will remain with her and grow as she grows. They will help to shape her into a caring and compassionate adult.

The Law, in whatever version each of us
knows it best, shows us the way
we should live our lives.

***The Promise is a personal statement
of endeavour rather than a creed
for exclusive membership.***

As a Guide I remember a Patrol Outdoor Challenge organised by local Scouts. The emphasis was on competition – there was a time limit with penalty points. There was some distance between the activities and on the way between two activities we noticed a man searching in the grass for something and looking distressed.

Our Patrol stopped and offered help, we searched for a couple of minutes without success then competition set in again and, with apologies, we raced off to the next activity. We all experienced guilt that we had not stayed to find the lost item.

At the end of the day we discovered – and expected – that we had lost the competition through time penalties. We were, however, given special commendation for being the only Patrol who had stopped to help the 'plant'.

Every Guide at that event learned something about her Promise to "help other people". I know I did.

**I still look for ways to help other people
without waiting to be asked.**

"My best" is now quite a strong faith but it was not always so. For a long time "my best" was to keep an open mind and at one time it was just to be prepared to listen.

There are times in our lives when even "my best" is not enough and we have to learn that it is sometimes not as good as our neighbour's poorest effort. This does not mean that I should, therefore, stop striving, but rather that I should accept that which I cannot change.

On a journey, the scenery is constantly changing, the hills and valleys, the urban and rural scenes. My life, too, presents changes. These sometimes demand positive action and sometimes careful listening. Throughout my journey I need to be alert to those changes.

I always try to do "my best" but believe that the best is yet to come.

It should be a promise that grows with us, not one we need to grow into.

A promise is something vibrant and living. It implies that a person makes a conscious effort to carry out what she has said she will do. It requires commitment and perseverance. Although some promises do relate to one-off events, many promises extend over and have implications for much of our lives.

Our Guide Promise, although made at one special event, is renewed on different occasions in our Guiding lives. Each time we renew it we are given the opportunity to reflect on what the Promise means to us now as we grow in our understanding of ourselves as people and as we travel along the Guiding road.

The Promise is like an acorn planted within us. One day it will become a majestic oak.

*If the girls do not know anything of God
when they come to us, this is our opportunity
to help them. As an outdoor Movement
we can show them God in the wonders of
nature and what better place and time
than camp or Pack Holiday.*

When we are out-of-doors, our senses are roused by the
space and freshness that is still in the world. Without the
routine of day-to-day living, we become, almost insensibly
at first, aware of the beauty of the landscape, of plants,
of birdsong. Our spirits lift, and there are, for many,
moments of joy and wonder.

At such times we can see and feel God in creation, and we
can speak of it, without embarrassment, to those who
share the experience.

**It is easy to see God in the living world
of the out-of-doors.**

***The Promise is a personal statement
of endeavour rather than a creed
for exclusive membership.***

There is nothing exclusive about Guiding; it is open to all girls and women who understand and are willing to make the Promise. Guiding places great value on the development of the individual, encouraging each member, according to her age and abilities, to become more independent, responsible and aware.

The Promise's code of behaviour, therefore, cannot be imposed, but seeks the active co-operation of each individual and an effort to 'do her best'. The commitment is a personal one, not an oath of allegiance to any club.

**Remembering my Promise, I will endeavour
to grow as an individual.**

***If the girls do not know anything of God
when they come to us, this is our opportunity
to help them. As an outdoor Movement
we can show them God in the wonders of
nature and what better place and time
than camp or Pack Holiday.***

No doubt each one of us has experienced a magical moment when we have realised the majesty of creation. It may have been when standing on the top of a mountain; noticing the delicate beauty but immense strength of a spider's web glistening with early morning dew; marvelling at the intricacy of a frosted window, or watching the skill of a bird in flight.

Camps, holidays, rambles, picnics, bonfire night, dawn hikes, all offer wonderful opportunities for us to pause and reflect on the miracles of the Creator's world, but we have to seize these fleeting moments and not wait for evening prayers of the Guide's Own.

Whoever you are with, children or other adults, just pause for a few moments' quiet reflection and help them to wonder in silence. These magic moments can be sufficient to have a profound effect and can often lead to some very heart-searching discussions about God and faith.

Treasure these moments, they last a lifetime.

Maybe we don't live our lives to the letter of the Promise, but we have a framework to guide us.

Coping with adolescence, both physically and emotionally, can be a demanding experience. Everyone tells you "The world is your oyster", "Make sure you get a good education", "You'll grow out of your acne" and "Just wait until the 'right' boy comes along!"

As a young woman, where is it possible to just 'be yourself' without comparison with the stereotypical teenager? Guiding offers such an environment, a place to grow emotionally and spiritually and to work out what you want from your life and not what others want of you.

The framework of the Promise is a commitment to follow a certain code of living which is like a personal piece of elastic – it lets you stretch yourself to your limit but is always strong and resilient and helps to keep you from going too far.

You alone set the direction of your life, Guiding offers you the protection of a piece of elastic to take with you.

Guiding gives us the blocks to build who we are.

The Promise was never meant to refer to Christians alone but to all with a faith in a supreme being.

Guiding is a world-wide Movement aimed at promoting the self-development of girls and young women. A fundamental part of our self is our spiritual self and for Guiding to fulfil its aim it must enable the girl to discover and develop her spiritual self.

The journey of discovery may take many routes, many twists and turns, but when a girl has found her spiritual path and seeks to follow its way, then Guiding has fulfilled one of its aims.

It does not matter then if the girl refers to the supreme being as Allah, God, YHWH, Buddha or Brahman.

I promise to love *my* God.

Perhaps it is how the Promise is applied to the Programme that should be looked at.

Whichever way you look at it, the Promise is central to the Programme, and lies at the heart of everything we do. Its values underpin our progress, influence our relationships and inform our choices. It enables us all to start from where we are, to develop at our own pace, and to 'do our best'.

Within the Programme, the Promise provides focus and cohesion. It ensures that we don't merely deliver a range of enjoyable activities, but that each and every activity provides an opportunity for the girl to reflect on her growing understanding of the Promise and its application for her life.

The Guider can prompt this reflection by asking, for example, "What do you think getting your first aid certificate has got to do with your Promise?", "What did you learn about yourself in the Patrol cooking competition?", "How did you feel when Emma told us she had taken drugs at a party?" or "Why did you stay behind after all the others had gone?"

As leaders, we have a responsibility to develop our skills as 'catalysts' to encourage real reflection which leads to growth. The challenge is to resist imposing our own values or provoking weighty discussion beyond the moral maturity of the young person.

As a Guider I use the Promise to link experience and reflection; through listening to each other, we all grow.

They like a "yes" to be a "yes" and a "no" a "no".

One of the characteristics of the very young is their ability to see things in absolute terms. A thing either 'is' or 'isn't'; they either 'will' or 'won't' do something; the world is divided into 'goodies' and 'baddies'.

It is only as a child begins to mature through adolescence that she realises that life doesn't always line up on one side or another – there are blurred edges and grey areas. She develops an understanding of another's point of view and the skills of consensus and compromise.

She also learns that some of her absolute values are only relative. She reaches true maturity when she is able to judge for herself those values which are immutable for her life.

I must not be so positive about *my* values that I don't allow others to develop their own.

God is God, regardless of the name by which He is known.

The major faiths of the world all acknowledge a supreme being, usually called by a form of 'God'. It seems unreasonable to say you believe in one God as Christian, but then deny that Allah, whom Muslims worship, exists and that they have it wrong.

Surely if someone believes in one God then it is reasonable to accept that there is only one God and that through historical, geographical and social evolution people from different ethnic backgrounds have come to worship Him (Her?) in a variety of ways.

Many of us who are fortunate to work with and have friends from other faiths constantly enrich our own faith by discovering how many of our beliefs are shared. For each of us, our God expects us to love and care for one another and accept that God is God regardless of how we worship Him.

By loving *my* God I can understand and respect the love that others have for *their* God.

*One is only able to pass on to young people
ideals and beliefs according to
one's own state of faith.*

This is true only if the 'ideals' and 'beliefs' one is trying to pass on concern only one's own faith – whatever state it is in.

Few leaders in the Guide Movement have real difficulty with the active and positive aspects of the Law, or with the need to encourage good citizenship as encompassed in 'Service to the Queen and other people'.

It is not unexpected that the most fundamental part of the Promise "to love my God" should give rise to the most heart-searching. Not unexpected and to be welcomed, for it is only by searching – your heart or conscience – that you find that for which you seek.

**Searching and seeking are what keep me going
on my spiritual journey.**

Slacken the guy ropes
but keep the tent pegs in.

Every good camper knows the nightly ritual of slackening the guy ropes in case of rain. Without this practical example of 'being prepared' there is a danger that the canvas will tear under the increased tension. But what an act of faith this is for new campers who need reassurance that the tent pegs will keep the structure safe and the tent will still be standing in the morning.

So it is with our Promise. Our young people need enough rope to be able to explore their faith and test out the views they hear around them so they can reach their own conclusions.

By 'pegging' this exploration within the safe environment of our rules for living – the Law – the balance between flexibility and security remains, and today's trusting Brownie, rebellious Guide and radical Ranger can mature into tomorrow's responsible and confident citizen with a 'structure' that will last her a lifetime, not just through the night.

**The Law is a secure framework through which
to live a full and worthwhile life.**

No one at the age of 11 knows all about God.
It takes a lifetime and one is still learning.
Like a lot of things.

In today's world many girls have not even heard that there is a God and often they are only faced with such a possibility when they join The Guide Association. Thus they have no, or at the very most a limited, experience of what it is to believe in a supernatural being. As Guiders we have a great responsibility in helping them to make their Promise and so start them on a lifetime of discovery.

In situations where a girl declares herself to be an atheist but wishes to make the Promise, an opportunity arises for the Guider to tackle the whole matter of faith, highlighting the quote at the beginning. Then even if the unit is distinctly Christian in both membership and leadership, encourage the girls, perhaps in Patrols, to discover for themselves something about other faiths as well as their own.

In this way both Guiders and girls will travel a little further on their own journey of faith.

Life is a journey of exploration
and much more enjoyable when we
'travel' with companions.

One of the things that makes the Guiding Programme
different from the Programmes of most other youth
organisations is its Promise and Law, with the concept of
God and the idea that achieving one's full potential
involves sharing and service.

Another difference is that the adult concerned is also
committed to the Promise and alert to the possibilities of
the Programme to raise awareness of a spiritual dimension
to life.

By working as part of a group, planning activities, taking
up challenges, young people can be helped to see
their own place in things. Camp on a lovely evening,
raising money for world issues, games that teach inner
disciplines – all the activities done each week – these are
the practical working out of the Promise.

All of this is implicit in the Programme: maybe we should
make it explicit more often. It is not just *what* we do but
how we do it.

The Promise makes all the difference.

Maybe we don't live our lives to the letter of the Promise, but we have a framework to guide us.

If we were to say that we always kept our Promise, surely we would be under an illusion? Just as each day we accept that there are ways that we could have 'tried harder', so we are assured that we can start afresh tomorrow. The Promise is a guide to measure our standards and attainments.

Taken in its simplistic form by a young member, it is a broad outline to work to, attainable with effort; for an older member with deeper understanding, the framework becomes more complex but still something to cling to.

The more sideshoots a climbing plant develops, the more it depends on a structure to support it. The more complex our lives become, the more we need a strong framework to work to.

The firm foundation of my Promise enables me to build with confidence.

The Promise and Law is a living force.

When I was asked to write about the Promise, my immediate reaction was "Oh no! I couldn't do that!" – but that reaction made me think. How often we *all* react like this whenever we are asked to look a little wider, try something new or different, accept a new challenge.

But you know, it is only in challenging ourselves that we grow into really useful, thoughtful, mature people.

And this is where our Promise comes in, as a very real spiritual support. I made my Promise as a Guide at the age of 11 as we all do. I remember the pleasure, excitement and anticipation of being welcomed with something really big.

As I grow older, I grow also to recognise the fuller significance of what I did when I made that Promise and I find that it becomes more and more relevant to the life I try to live.

By helping others to explore their understanding of the Promise, we discover more about our own.

*Every leader training should be
a 'Promise and Law training'
without being labelled as such.*

The basis of Guiding is the Five Essential Elements. These are what makes Guiding special.

Guiding is something you feel – it's about respect, attitudes, values, caring, being, sharing and doing.

Through the Five Essentials, training explains, clarifies and supports all leaders in the delivery of high quality experiences, activities and opportunities. The Five Essentials cannot, and should not, be boxed or separated one from another: they are interdependent.

It should be understood by leaders that all training for their Guiding has at its basis the Promise and Law.

**The Promise and Law is there, in action,
in all our Guiding activities.**

The Promise should be demanding or it is irrelevant.

When we do something which is too easy it can become boring.

When we are ironing, we find ways of occupying our minds at the same time: talking to the family, watching TV, listening to music – anything to keep our minds busy while our hands carry out a routine task.

It is amazing how quickly a group of Guiders can wash up for a large number! They are not concentrating on the task, but on their conversation: yet the job is done thoroughly because it is undemanding.

We all thrive on challenges: they stretch us intellectually and physically, keeping us alert and involved in the activity. Guiding is about challenges. We try to help the girls to think for themselves and also outside themselves.

The most demanding challenge for the young is to work out for themselves what life is all about. Why are we here? Why is the world like this? What can we do to improve it?

The Promise is designed to help them to think about these issues which are demanding for all of us. If the girls engage with them, then they will not see the Promise as boring or irrelevant.

**The Promise must challenge us
if it is to be effective.**

Guiding has played an important part in my life, especially its values and aims. I strongly feel that it has made me the person I am today and that has been based around the Promise I made.

As we grow our lives are affected by our environment, the people we meet and the experiences we have. Making the Promise as a child gives us values to live up to and helps us shape into responsible and caring adults.

The Guide Movement is also full of women who display the Promise in action and become rôle models for those who come into contact with them.

I can think of times when I have followed a course of action guided by the words of the Promise and the example set me by other members of the Movement. This is what makes The Guide Association a force to be reckoned with.

Guiding changes lives.

One of the easiest ways to discuss the 'God bit' is out-of-doors.

We accept that God is central to our Promise and Law and we accept God as our Creator. The out-of-doors brings us nearer to God.

The smallest green shoot and first snowdrop – a promise of spring after the long winter. Standing on top of a mountain having struggled to the summit gives a feeling of self-achievement, and confidence in those who have encouraged you on the way.

It is not always easy to keep our Promise and Law, but it is the 'struggle' of coming through that makes it all worthwhile.

**To enjoy anything worthwhile in life,
there should be a degree of difficulty in obtaining it.**

*It is fascinating to look back along the way
we've come in adjusting and adapting
to changes in society – and to try to look
forward in a way which keeps the roots.*

Guiding began with ideas which were ahead of their time, and has always been in the forefront of educational thinking and methods. It has made an immense contribution to communities everywhere, through two World Wars and in peacetime. It has had a significant effect on the status of women throughout the world, and today there are millions of young people for whom Guiding has made a difference.

As we plan for a new millennium in this age of technology, the world is very different from that of 1910 when Girl Guides officially started, yet the fundamental values and principles will be as valid in years to come as they were then. These ideals, embodied in the Promise and Law, are what makes Guiding extra-special.

**The values of my Promise stand firm
in an ever-changing world.**

*Guiding has played an important part
in my life, especially its values and aims.
I strongly feel that it has made me the person
I am today and that has been based
around the Promise I made.*

Never having been a Brownie or a Guide, I first made my Promise as an adult leader 15 years ago.

Over these years I have become increasingly aware of the impact that these words have had on my life. I often recall my Promise during everyday occurrences. Where I would have said "I can't", I will now meet the challenge; if I think ill of someone it is only a temporary thought as my Promise shoots into mind; I try to make a conscious effort to help someone in need even if it is not always a convenient time.

Guiding has changed my life. I made a Promise and I will do my best to keep it.

**The Promise and Law is a code of action
which directs my journey through life.**

*Guiders should not commit themselves
to traditions but to Guiding;
you cannot guide today's young people
with yesterday's values and traditions.*

Guiding is for the girl – there would be unanimous agreement on that. What is the 'girl' of today? She is a global citizen – in the era of mass communication she is shaped by the influence of many different cultures: from the food she eats, to the clothes she wears or the games she plays.

In the multicultural world in which we live, Guiding can celebrate the diversity around us by exploring all that is happening and providing us with the life-skills to make discoveries for ourselves.

As leaders we have to start from where girls and young women are – that means we may have to consider our own position; we may even need to catch the girls up before we can really begin the journey of life discovery together.

**I listen to the voices of today's young women
and discover that some of my cherished values
turn out to be outworn prejudices.**

*The job of an adult leader is to provide
a sound base from which to question.*

I would like to think that no one would repeat the Guide Promise and Law without thinking about what she was saying, but young people need to feel confident about themselves before they will start to question their beliefs.

It is never easy for parents and leaders to stand back and allow those in our charge to query that which we have taught, but it is necessary to allow young people to develop as they go through phases of discovery about themselves.

**I should have the confidence to question
my own beliefs before I can accept
questions from others.**

*I accept that girls often repeat it by rote,
not really thinking of what it means
and how it applies to them.*

There are a number of different ways of learning. One of the most common is to learn by rote. Our 'times tables', dates in history or a religious creed are often learned at an early age and can be recited without thought many years later.

Learning the words of the Promise and Law is not difficult. The rôle of the Guider is to assist the girls in reaching an understanding in order that they can apply what they have learned to their everyday lives.

The most successful form of learning involves the use of all our senses. Ask the girls to represent the Promise or Law as pictures, or a sketch or mime. Suggest they write a story including each Clause of the Law or look for examples of the Promise and Law in action in books or newspaper articles.

Each girl will have a different interpretation. A discussion, led by a Guider, will help the words to become meaningful, whether learned by rote or not.

**It's not important how we learn;
what's important is that we understand.**

*If one starts with God one can progress
to the spiritual value of what God means
and what it means to the child.*

We sometimes refer to God as 'Father', someone who cares for us, protects and loves us. Youngsters will relate to such a figure for whom they can show their love by doing their best to keep the Guide Promise and Law.

As we mature we discover that God's love for us is not dependent upon our reciprocal love. He loves us anyway.

This realisation of the nature of God's "love that passeth all understanding" is the beginning of a true spiritual relationship.

**Though I may not always love my God,
He always, unfailingly, loves me.**

As the girls grow so they understand more what the Promise means. I do so agree with the statement; it is 'a framework for knowing and a springboard for growing'.

It is the very heart of Guiding. It beats away every moment, reminding us of the vows we have made. It helps to pump new life into our daily routine, just as the heart pumps nourishment through our bodies.

It provides the backbone to our commitment, holding together the different strands of our lives and, like a skeleton, it gives us a flexible framework within which we can explore the living world.

I live and grow with my Promise.

It is fascinating to look back along the way we've come in adjusting and adapting to changes in society – and to try to look forward in a way which keeps the roots.

So many things have made the practicality of life easier – domestic appliances, fast food, travel, information technology – to name a few. Old disciplines seem no longer relevant; the washing cycle has been reduced from days to a few hours; spring cleaning is accomplished at any time of the year; letters are dispensed with in favour of the telephone or fax machine.

The practical disciplines I learned as a Guide related to the climate of the 1950s. We need to look at the 1990s, indeed forward to the 21st century and encourage Guides in disciplines relevant to them.

What is unchanged, what really matters, is the discipline of learning to love my God, concerning myself with the community (local and global) and making the most of myself. That endeavour ensures the roots are constant.

If I can be true to my Promise, the future need hold no fears.

One of the most rewarding things about our rôle as Guiders must be to see the girls 'growing within their Promises'.... They are so full of surprises and we have some very deep-thinking young people these days.

Young girls frequently amaze us by their somewhat startling, thought-provoking questions – "Can angels eat?", "Why doesn't the sun fall down?" – and the rather surprising, matter-of-fact, yet satisfying answers for such ponderable and seemingly unanswerable enquiries when they are encouraged to think these through for themselves. These indicate just how they test and deal with the challenges and interpretation of the world in which they live.

Observing young 'me-centred' egocentric girls develop into independent, confident and sociable individuals is always a rewarding, yet salutary, experience.

Children grow in understanding of their Promise when we give them time and space to explore, question and make their own response to the world in which they live.

*A promise can neither assist
nor hinder anything. Carrying out a promise
may well do so.*

Making a promise, however seriously, is of itself no more
than an isolated act, a declaration of intent. It is not until
the words are put into action that they come truly alive.

Carrying out a promise may be inconvenient or downright
difficult, but it is the actions and words – or the refusal to
act and silence – that fulfil our Promise and affect our lives
and those of others.

**It is not through making a promise,
but through keeping it, that I show my worth as
a person and as a Guide.**

We did not join The Guide Association. We are the Guide Movement. We wanted it, we started it and we go on making it work.

We know that within Guiding we can find hope, security, friendship, adventure and many other things which we can find nowhere else. To a large extent this comes from the caring and the example handed on from one generation to the next and one girl to another.

It comes also from the knowledge that we *are* the Guide Movement. Me, the girl up the road, the girl from France who came to camp, the girls we sent toys to in the Sudan.

We all make basically the same Promise at six or 60, which is a Promise for life.

Once a Guide, always a Guide.

The point of the Promise has to be that one's depth of understanding increases as one progresses through the Movement.

As we travel through our journey of life we gain experience and knowledge, broadening our horizons and becoming witnesses to all that is growing. Our understanding of life becomes greater and our knowledge grows.

This is similar to a single flower in a field which spreads its seeds bringing forth flowers in greater numbers, spreading out until the field is full. However, like the flowers some of our knowledge becomes clouded and wilts away, leaving space for new flowers and greater understanding to grow.

As we grow, understanding grows.

*The only person – except God – who can know
how far you have progressed is yourself.*

During my fifth year at school I attended an Outward
Bound course. The three-week course comprised many
activities – walking, camping, tree-climbing and canoeing
to name a few – and in all of these things we were gently
'bullied' by our instructors to push ourselves to our limits.

There was one activity, however, where we were told it
was up to us as to whether we participated. The activity
was to jump into the plunge pool of the waterfall in Glen
Nevis. We had to jump right into the heart of the water, for
to go too far would mean we would crash into the lip of
the pool. Standing on the edge of the ledge above the
waterfall I knew that, although I was terrified, this was the
real test of the three weeks.

I *did* jump, and experienced a unique feeling, the cold
water electrifying and invigorating me. I knew then that I
had progressed and would go home a different person
from the one who had arrived three weeks earlier.

**Only in pushing myself do I discover
what I can really do.**

The Promise is the Association's 'ace' card.

That's quite a claim isn't it? The ace card is the one that beats all others, is envied and sought after by those who don't have it and is often produced with a flourish by those who do! Equally, think of an ace in tennis, the ultimate serve, or the accolade given to an ace pilot.

Whichever way you look at it, the word 'ace' denotes something very special, something to be proud of and not something to keep to yourself.

Equally, we should be proud of our Promise and all it stands for and not be embarrassed or apologetic. To achieve this we need to discuss it openly so that all our members are comfortable with it being a normal part of everyday life. Then we too will be able to produce our ace with a flourish and win in the game of life.

Let's lay our cards on the table and be proud of the Promise and all it represents.

Girls are with us primarily for fun, friendship
and learning in a caring environment.
As they enjoy Guiding, the Guiders use
the foundation of the Promise to encourage
physical, mental and spiritual growth.

It is amazing what can be done under the disguise of fun and games to assist the mental and spiritual growth of the girls who are with us. I remember a particular problem of relationships at camp slowly coming to rights through a determined choice of themes for daily prayers, and through careful choice of games and activities and, more particularly, their organisation.

The essence, as always in Guiding, is in having fun and enjoyment because of the way things are done rather than simply in the activity itself. It is often later in life that realisation comes of the value of the Guiding Method. That realisation comes more readily if the memories are of enjoyment.

What I do may be fun,
but how I do it makes it special.

It should be a Promise that grows with us, not one we need to grow into.

Our Promise allows individual interpretation and is not written in stone, but is a building block, a code for life which increases our understanding and enjoyment of daily experiences.

As experiences change, the interpretation of the code will also develop, adding new meaning to the initial words spoken.

A Guider is responsible for creating opportunities and supporting the girls while they mature and grow in accordance with the Law.

Guiding belongs to the girls of today. It is up to us as their Guiders to see that they have fun living by a code *they* understand.

One of the easiest ways to discuss the 'God bit' is out-of-doors.

Indoors, we are surrounded by human creativity: walls, furniture, a television set. Outside, we are surrounded by what we may plant and nurture, but cannot create.

Both our delight in our surroundings and our realisation of our limitations provide us with opportunities to talk about God in our world and in our lives.

Being outside in the created world can help us to speak openly of our true beliefs.

> *The job of an adult leader is to provide a*
> *sound base from which to question.*

An important feature in a young woman's life is a sense of belonging, of feeling secure. Many girls and young women will have only part of this feeling provided by their family environment and many will seek to make up the shortfall by their experiences with their peers. Guiding has an important rôle to play here for all girls and young women.

The rôles of the leader are varied and include supporter, friend, listener, teacher, mentor. Indirectly you are responsible for shaping the lives of the girls and young women with whom you work and this can be a powerful position.

The Guiding Method ensures you do not abuse that power, since your energies are directed at enabling the girls and young women to seek out the answers for themselves. As leaders you provide them with a safety net and an acceptance without question of who they are – individuals with their own emerging identities.

In posing the questions, I realise it is not necessarily my rôle to provide the answers.

*The Promise and Law provides
a tangible sense of fellowship and oneness
with Guides world-wide.*

It is so hurtful, especially if we are young, to feel that a promise made has been broken. Even though it may have been quite trivial, it was felt to be part of a bargain which was not kept.

Our Promise is made by each of us, willingly and without conditions. The words of the Promise are similar for all Girl Guides and Girl Scouts and express a shared purpose and commitment by girls and women around the world who gladly intend to do their best, to love their God, and to serve their country or community. This gives a powerful image of a source for good, for self-fulfilment and for progress.

As travellers on life's journey it is a wonderful experience to meet Guides anywhere in the world and to feel immediate rapport with them. There is spontaneous recognition and understanding of all that we share and have in common.

**When I meet a Guide from anywhere in the world,
I meet a friend.**

*To make a promise is to give a commitment
and our first commitment is to 'do our best'.*

How thankful I am that our Founder asked us to promise to 'do our best' and not 'be the best' or always succeed! If the latter had been the case I would have failed to live up to the ideals of Guiding many times over.

Likewise we must remember that we are asking each individual to 'do *her* best' and that 'best' may be quite different from the next girl.

This isn't to say that we have dual standards, quite the contrary. Our standard is the same for everyone – we must all strive to fulfil our full potential.

This concept is particularly important when it comes to the Law. I have often heard Guiders say that we shouldn't expect our members to be all the qualities asked for in the Law, all the time.

The answer is quite simply that I agree. But I *do* expect everyone to 'do her best'.

**The Promise sets a challenging standard
that is within everyone's reach.**

We live in an increasingly secularised world.
Surely this makes it even more important that
we try to help the young people we serve to
recognise, to know and to love their Creator.

It is sometimes thought that God can only be served through organised religion and that absence from corporate worship implies lack of faith.

Young people of today may give that impression more and more, as they become increasingly dissatisfied with the lack of relevance to them of the styles of corporate worship on offer. Their faith, however, should not be underestimated by adults and it needs nurturing and encouraging in a sensitive way.

Today's judgements should not be based on yesterday's standards: each individual should be cherished and encouraged to know and love her Creator. Perhaps our job is to put a lie to the statement that we live in an increasingly secular world.

I promise that I will do my best to love my God.

A Guide faces challenge and learns from her experiences.

A challenge is the setting of a goal which can be achieved through sustained effort. Life holds many challenges for us all – some we choose and some are thrust upon us. As Guides we are challenged through the Promise to try to be a particular kind of person. It is a challenge which can be achieved through sustained effort but which can continuously be reset.

An athlete or climber sets to work keenly to get herself into peak condition for her planned event. She doesn't decide upon her challenge and then forget about it until a day or two before it is due to take place. Her goal is set and she strives to achieve it, living by that goal day by day determined to give of her best.

Thus it should be with the challenge of the Guide Promise, practising and working at it day by day.

**The Promise reflects an ideal I can achieve
if I keep on trying.**

*God is God, regardless of the name
by which He is known.*

There are many religions and each has a very different concept of the 'divine being' they worship, who may or may not be called God. The different religions are not basically the same, although they might share similar teachings.

In Islam the term 'Allah' translates into 'the God' meaning supreme being, whilst in Judaism the name of God is considered too holy to be spoken and so the word 'YHWH' is used, which translated, equates to the name God used for himself when making a covenant with Israel, namely 'I AM'.

When Christians wish to speak of God, they use terms which illustrate the various aspects of God as they understand Him, for example, 'Father', 'Holy Spirit' and 'Lord'. Hindus have many Gods.

So, when a member of the Association makes a promise to 'my God', each according to her faith will have her own vision of what 'God' means.

**Will I ever begin to grasp this awesome truth:
the great 'I AM' – infinite in mercy, love,
wisdom and understanding – knows
and calls me by my name?**

*One is only able to pass on to young people
ideals and beliefs according to
one's own state of faith.*

Guiding is a way of life. Everyone has their own spiritual pathway to travel on through life. In Guiding we must respect the right of the individual to follow her own pathway to the best of her ability.

The Guide Promise and Law is there to help us, and to guide us on our own chosen pathway. As a Christian I take as my guide the words of Christ taken from St Matthew's Gospel and understand them to say to me: "Whatever you do for the least of my brethren, you do it for me".

In keeping my Guide Promise to be helpful, friendly, kind and considerate to other people, I am doing it for Christ, to Christ. Thus my baptismal vows and church laws are complemented by my Guide Promise and Law and together they are my way of life.

**The beliefs we hold and the promises we make
help form the people we are.**

We know it's hard to keep the Promise, but we
want to have something to try for.

We, of the human race were given flesh and blood, bones and brains, and a spirit living in us. Some were not given very good flesh and blood, bones and brains, but were given the same spirit living within.

Often it is our spirit that keeps us going when our body cries to give up. Making a promise is rather like that spirit. A promise can keep you going when you think of giving up. Having spirit is a joyous thing and sometimes a nuisance. Keeping a promise is a joyous thing and sometimes a nuisance.

You cannot believe you have a spirit if you have no faith. You cannot believe in someone's promise to you, if you have no faith.

Listen to yourself making your Guide Promise and remember your spiritual Father who has put His faith in you to keep it.

Have faith in all who make the Guide Promise,
especially those who make their Promise
to us as leaders. Trust them.

I know most children make their Promise 'parrot-fashion'. I did, but something sticks. Through working together, playing together, growing together, they come to know something of the meaning of the Promise, which has been our foundation.

While the Guide Programme rightly puts the Promise as the central important aspect of Guiding it is not, however, the main reason for girls joining. They probably come because their friends are members and it is only later, even perhaps after they have left Guides, that the Promise and its meaning becomes truly important.

That is why the Guider talking through the Promise and discussing each part is so valuable. A young person's clear vision makes this a privilege.

Once the words are learned, the meaning of the Promise can truly be discovered.

*Guiders should not commit themselves
to traditions but to Guiding;
you cannot guide today's young people
with yesterday's values and traditions.*

When Guiding started, society was totally different from
the society in which we live today. B-P started Guiding in
a climate of war, strict discipline and nationalism. The
military-style uniform, words such as 'honour' and 'duty',
activities such as marching and semaphore were well
understood and accepted in the context of that time.

However, although these traditional words and activities
are no longer relevant to girls in the context of our time,
the values embodied in the Promise and Law are. 'To love
and serve God and to love and serve your neighbour' are
still relevant today and they still will be into the 21st
century. They are just expressed in a different way.

Girls in today's society are concerned with helping
children in Bosnia, making up Peace Packs, cleaning
rivers, preserving endangered species, raising funds for
the homeless.

So let us reflect on ways to help today's girls to build on
the timeless values of the Promise and Law.

**Involvement in the concerns of today
is an expression of the timeless Promise and Law.**

The interpretation of the Promise is the Guider's main duty.

Yes, interpreting the Promise is the Guider's main duty but it is not the same duty as that of a teacher teaching the 'two times table'.

Our duty is to the spirit of Guiding, helping the new recruit and enrolled member understand the core values expressed in our Promise. Our duty then is really our privilege, sharing with girls and women something of the vision of B-P; enabling them to catch that vision for themselves; journeying with them as they develop a personal faith in God and a sense of responsible citizenship.

Interpreting the Promise as Guiders is not a one-way process but one where we all learn from each other. I am challenged by my seven-year-old Brownies and they are challenged as they work through their pre-Promise book.

As a Guider, I am privileged to share the Promise with others. This leads to greater understanding for all.

Once words are learned, their meaning can deepen throughout life. If someone does learn something by heart, that suggests it is meaningful to them.

It depends how things are learned in the first place, for example many who have crammed for exams have totally forgotten most of the knowledge almost as soon as the paper is finished.

It requires enthusiasm on the part of the Guider when encouraging the girl to learn the Promise and Law by heart, so that they become valued concepts rather than words which have to be repeated 'parrot-fashion' in order to join 'the club'.

When a girl sees that the words mean a lot to the Guider then she too will not only want to learn them by heart, but wish to understand them for herself.

Each time I look at a picture I see something new. So it is with my Promise.

Whatever denomination, religion or faith we cannot hope to find spiritual values on our own merits – we must accept the intervention of the spiritual being we are seeking.

Spiritual values are those which add another dimension to our lives. No longer do we live just in time and space, but we have access to something much greater. This gives us a wider view, a deeper resource. We have a companion on our way through life, to whom we can refer when tough decisions have to be made, with whom we can share our joys and sorrows.

The acceptance of a spiritual being within us completes us, makes us a whole person, without taking away our freedom to choose. Seeking this being, following a spiritual path, is part of our journey through life.

We need a map of some description – we cannot do it completely on our own. In the spiritual world within us we can find the way ahead, and travel it in company with others – those whose example we cherish, or those who follow the same path now.

Be still, and find God within you, around you and in the people you meet.

> *The young people of today, more than ever before, need something definite to hold on to.*

Can you remember how exciting it is to be eight, 12 or 14? Your whole life before you, new experiences and adventures around every corner and not a care in the world! Really? If that was your experience, great, but many of our young people will also have to cope with the pressure to conform, to try smoking, drugs, joy-riding, or whatever, and the bullying if they refuse, or are seen to be different.

To help them steer a course through this pressure and uncertainty they need the stability and security offered by our common-sense 'guide for life', our Promise and Law. This gives them a reference point of responsible behaviour against which to test any activities they are tempted to try.

Hence it is a code of what we should do, not a restrictive list of what we must not do: a help not a hindrance.

The 'guide for life' makes a Guide for life!

We all need to have the opportunity to think things through.

It is very easy to act on impulse, to judge somebody on first impressions, or to say something rash. Sometimes, our 'gut reaction' is correct but we always need to look beyond the surface in order to confirm our initial opinion or be able to change or modify it. An impressive speaker who talks with conviction can persuade us towards their viewpoint, but we need to be able to stand back and judge their statements objectively, often by seeking out and considering other points of view.

Before committing myself to making a promise or taking on responsibility, it is important to take time to consider the implications that making this promise would have.

In this way I learn to evaluate my own commitments and can decide whether I will fulfil what I set out to do.

I am an activist; I need to develop the patience and wisdom to wait and think before rushing in.

Everyone's concept of God is different.

It seems strange that most Guiders will agree with this statement yet be very wary or fearful of talking about their own concepts of God. These fears may be based on their own uncertainty about what they believe.

Many assume that others must be sure about their beliefs and have stronger convictions, and these Guiders therefore feel afraid of seemingly being less knowledgeable, or incompetent.

Everyone in leadership rôles, particularly Trainers and Guiders, must be prepared to acknowledge that they don't have the answers any more than anyone else, and that there are no right or wrong beliefs in who or what God is. No one, however confident or dogmatic, can prove that what they believe is right and that others are wrong.

One of the wonderful things about belonging to Guiding is that the Promise acknowledges the right of everyone to follow their faith and try to love and serve their God, however this is perceived. What must be encouraged is open, honest discussion without enforcement of personal beliefs on others.

**My God is to me what your God is to you,
the same though different.**

The only person – except God – who can know how far you have progressed is yourself.

We each make our Promise willingly and unconditionally. The words mean different things to us at different stages of our lives. As our vision grows so too can the meaning of the words.

However, 'doing our best' is something that we alone can judge, and talk over with our God. Others may help and encourage us, for instance to try harder in order to achieve, but in the end only we know for sure whether or not we have lived up to our perceptions of ourselves as individuals.

It is sometimes hard to acknowledge that things haven't worked out as we should have liked... the outcomes have been a disappointment, and all this in spite of doing our best in the circumstances... and then we have to trust that God knows that too.

There are no others but us. There never has been, and we, with all our imperfections, are needed to live out our Promise in the best way we can, because only then will it become a power for good.

Do your best for God and yourself.

***There are times of doubt, denial and
questioning... but the ability to hang on to the
knowledge that we are God's creatures will, in
the end, result in positive growth.***

Life would be easy if our spiritual growth were as
predictable as our physical development – infancy,
childhood, adolescence and maturity. Our beliefs and
values, our faith and hope would grow as we grew; there
would be no dark doubts and the questions of faith would
be resolved by our steady growth in understanding.

Life, however, isn't like that and the spiritual journey that
we all travel is marked along the way with doubts, denials,
disbelief and even despair.

Our limited human minds are not designed to fathom the
reasons why the unacceptable happens; what we do have,
however, is the capacity to believe in a loving Creator God
who cares for us all.

Instead of using energy to rail against God, we do better if
we concentrate on developing our faith in Him, and using
it to support us through the bad times, knowing that they
won't last for ever.

**Whilst I don't pretend to understand it,
I *do* believe there *is* a reason why.**

Slacken the guy ropes
but keep the tent pegs in.

Any camper knows that guy ropes need to be adjusted to respond to changes of wind and weather, but if the tent pegs come out the tent collapses.

In our lives, some of our attitudes and habits have to be flexible enough to adapt to changed conditions; but if we are to retain our integrity and value as people we must retain those beliefs and ideals which are fundamental to us.

We can compromise on passing and unimportant things, but not on matters of principle.

In your Promise you have a yardstick to measure things by.

Many of us, when we were little, went off to school or to play with the words "Be a good girl", ringing in our ears. We often translated this to ourselves as, "Don't get into trouble".

As we grow older we realise that it's more complicated than this.

In the world of today it is sometimes hard to tell good from bad without something to measure by.

The Promise gives us just this: a way of judging things, and deciding from that how we should act.

The Promise helps us decide how best to act.

The only person – except God – who can know how far you have progressed is yourself.

This implies a ruthless, no-holds-barred examination of my own beliefs and the way I respond to them.

I should not be too harsh a judge, although perhaps I should judge myself more harshly than I judge others.

It is sometimes my lot to be mis-judged by others. Then is the time for me to take comfort in the thought that God knows of my efforts and then I can honestly review my progress.

Life provides endless opportunities for me to review my progress; I should use them all and learn from the experience.

The context of a Guide gathering is one which supports and encourages many to gain strength and a feeling of worth.

I was one of a group of Rangers, Young Leaders and Guiders who recently visited Romania on a humanitarian aid trip. Our task whilst there was to paint and decorate four classrooms for children with special needs and to play with the children in the orphanage of the mountain village in which we were based.

During the many months of preparation I became increasingly apprehensive about how I would deal with whatever I might encounter. How would I react to the children and their appalling conditions? Would I be able to cope with my emotions? Would I come up with what was expected of me? However, all these fears proved groundless. As a group, we worked hard together, we cried and laughed together, we shared our fears and anxieties and all returned from Romania much richer for the experience.

We all have our own opinions, standards and values, but the friendliness of Guiding in general gives us a firm foundation to *try* to help others, share confidences and build very special bonds of friendship despite any differences we may have, because of our shared activities and work within the Movement.

None of us is as strong as all of us.

'We tend to go for the spirit of the thing'. How can we go for the spirit of something if we do not know what it is?

Coming to terms with the spirit of Guiding is about accepting that this is an element of Guiding which is intangible – it cannot be qualified, organised or measured. It is an aspect of personal growth which is enriching for all who experience it and yet can evade description.

A dawn hike to the summit of a mountain with a small group, with a moment of reflection and solitude on arrival can be a powerful experience. In pausing to look at the natural world around you, in comparison with the earth, sky and water, who are you, but a small insignificant human being?

By contrast, around a campfire in the evening, sitting huddled together for warmth and making music can generate a feeling of sheer happiness which is hard to define or explain in physical terms.

There can be a feeling for an individual at such times of being watched over, cared for by a higher spiritual being.

The important thing is you cannot touch these moments – they are part of a personal experience. Guiding creates these opportunities.

The human spirit of Guiding is the reflection of the divine spirit of the Creator.

> *You can imagine how touched I was
> this morning when one of my ex-Brownies,
> a very disruptive girl, and one who
> wouldn't go into Guides, arrived at church
> on her own. She spoke to me and
> said, "Part of my Promise, Brown Owl".*

This surely is what Guiding is all about. Our job is to sow the seeds, even if we are not privileged to see the fruit. The 'seed' may be a love of the outdoors, a chance at leadership or simply an introduction to a new activity.

But the most important must surely be a personal faith in God. This seed needs careful nurturing, perhaps the occasional pruning and the right amount of food for its particular stage of development, so that it is not forced. Equally it must be allowed to develop in its own way. No amount of attention will make a tomato grow into a rose!

So each girl should be supported in the development of her own faith, at her own pace and not be expected to conform to ours. After all, we're all still growing too!

The Promise helps the seed of faith to grow.

*I accept that girls often repeat it by rote,
not really thinking of what it means
and how it applies to them.*

Older members of the Association will remember that in their schooldays nearly everything taught had to be learned by heart and repeated by rote, for example, their 'times tables'. How they could be applied came afterwards.

However, they provided a very firm foundation which made the application that much easier. Somehow the oft-repeated words had been absorbed into one's very being. So it can be with the Promise and Law.

But if you are worried, try getting the girls to repeat them, putting the emphasis on different words each time. For example, highlighting the pronouns will underline the personal aspect of the Promise, whilst accentuating the verbs will highlight the action to be taken.

In this way you translate rote into meaning.

**Though I may learn the words of the Promise
by rote, my understanding of its meaning
for my life deepens daily.**

*I consider the Promise to be an excellent rule
for living a decent life. If one puts God first,
other people next and oneself last,
one cannot go very far wrong.*

The wonderful thing about the basic fundamentals of Guiding as set out by its Founder is that they are the basis for living a decent, reputable life and as such are acceptable to people of all faiths.

They have thus been adopted by women and girls around the world, adapting the Programme to suit their environment but following the principles of the Promise and the teaching of their God.

No one need feel ashamed of her beliefs. They all have much in common and are the basis for a happy life.

**Each time I renew our Promise I re-affirm
my commitment to a way of life that brings love
and understanding of others, especially
my sisters in Guiding.**

*Guiding has played an important part
in my life, especially its values and aims.
I strongly feel that it has made me the person
I am today and that has been based
around the Promise I made.*

As I grow older my understanding of the Promise becomes far more meaningful. In each stage of life, as in each section of Guiding, the Promise and Law has relevance for our age and understanding.

When I was younger everything was clear, everything was right or wrong. If it was right, I felt good and if it was wrong, I felt sorry. The older I become the more difficult it becomes to be so clear – there are too many shades of grey.

The Promise helps me to meet this change, to become more tolerant of myself as well as others and to know that it is not so much the deed which is right or wrong but the intention.

**When I decide what to do I ask myself
if the 'ideal Guide' would have done it.**

> *Maybe we don't live our lives to the letter of the Promise, but we have a framework to guide us.*

When we make our Promise, we say that we will 'do our best' and this is a recognition of human frailty. The framework provided by the Promise and Law tells us what sort of people we aspire to be.

It is a tough set of criteria that we have set before us and we probably all fail on at least one criterion every day. For example, we promise "to serve the Queen and my country".

A partial interpretation of this is that we are seeking to be good citizens, which means obeying the law of the land. When did you last try to sneak an extra mile or two an hour over the 70 mph speed limit on the motorway because you were late? When did you last use your employer's photocopier for papers to do with Guiding without paying for such use? When we do these actions, we know, deep down, that we shouldn't and that, therefore we are breaking our Promise.

Thus we recognise this and decide to do better next time. If we didn't exhibit such human fallibility we would be horrendously self-righteous little madams!

The framework of the Promise sets us standards to live by.

'We tend to go for the spirit of the thing'. How can we go for the spirit of something if we do not know what it is?

To me, the spirit of the Promise is not in the words themselves, but in the meaning behind them. Guides around the world do not all say an identical Promise but, in spirit, they mean the same thing.

As a Brownie, my leaders explained the meaning of the Promise to me. The words they used were simple for me to understand and their actions taught me by example. As I've grown older I've used different words to explain the Promise, but the spirit behind these words remains the same.

When I say my Promise, I mean that I will try to be the best person that I can, whether measured by my God, my neighbour or myself.

**Other people helped me to understand
the spirit of the Promise. Now, in my turn,
I will pass on that understanding.**

*A true sense of belonging must be
more than just the wearing of a badge or
payment of a subscription.*

Anyone can put on the outward signs of belonging to an organisation, although they probably wouldn't do so if they didn't want to belong.

However, being truly part of something involves more than outward signs.

To belong to Guiding means sharing the beliefs and standards that lie at the heart of it, and we should not only aim to do that ourselves, but help others to do so.

**I belong to Guides not through outward signs,
but through accepting and living up to
what is important to Guiding.**

A Guide is a good friend and a sister to all Guides. Sister is not an old-fashioned word and goes beyond friend. It emphasises the link in Guiding world-wide.

These links emphasise a basic principle: when Guides meet, they do so on common ground and are like a family with different relatives, such as the Scouts.

Indeed, Guiding is a world-wide umbrella which covers every race, colour and religion and has no prejudices.

The links of my Guiding sisterhood connect me in love and give me greater understanding of all women everywhere.

Although I don't recall the exact circumstances of making my Promise, I still tingle when I share it with a new Guide, or when we renew it together, because I feel it is the one unifying aspect of Guiding around the world and across the ages.

I never cease to wonder at the international aspect of Guiding. The thought that I could travel the world, crossing numerous so-called cultural boundaries and yet find instant friendship amongst like-minded women amazes me! This is one of the strengths of Guiding, made possible by our acceptance of unity despite diversity.

But this diversity doesn't just cover our sisters abroad. Each of our members is a unique individual with different needs when it comes to understanding the Promise. As Guiders we have to help her explore the meaning of the Promise and put it into practice so that it becomes a living creed, not just a gateway to receiving a badge.

So relate your Programme to the Promise as well as the Eight Points and help your unit share that special tingle and bond.

Guiding is very special and the Promise helps keep it that way.

Familiar words learned by heart will grow in meaning as we mature. At any level of maturity we can only promise according to our understanding and experience of those words.

We have all had to learn some things by heart, be it 'times tables', spelling rules ('i' before 'e' except after 'c'), poems ("If you can keep your head when all about you/Are losing theirs and blaming it on you..."), irregular verbs (je suis, tu es, il est...). At the time, when we had to learn them, we did not always fully understand them – perhaps we still do not! But with maturity and experience, we come to assimilate what we have learned and it becomes part of us, there to be drawn upon when necessary.

This assimilation is helped by using and talking about the material we have learned. If we provide opportunities for girls to talk about their understanding of the Promise and Law and to play games which require them to think about the implications, then their understanding will be expanded.

Regular opportunities are built into the Programme for Guiders to talk to their girls about the Promise; these are important and should not be rushed if the girls are to find the words growing in meaning.

As I grow in experience, so my understanding of the familiar grows.

> *More people are thinking about it*
> *in a personal way as it affects them*
> *and their life.... I believe this is a good sign*
> *and shows that individuals are really*
> *searching and exploring what the Promise*
> *means for them – now.*

A promise, as we are taught as children, is a personal and binding undertaking. However, today's young people are encouraged to ask questions – not just to accept matters as previous generations have been accustomed to do. We are all much more aware of our rights as individuals.

Perhaps this has prompted many to probe into the true meaning of the parts of the Promise and Law as they relate to us.

My commitment to the Promise encourages
me to review the direction of my life.

*Looking further into the clauses of the Law,
the more often I read them, the more I grew
to like them and understand them. In fact
I was quite excited by them.*

It is said that familiarity breeds contempt but this is not always true. I am sure we can all think of words – perhaps a poem, a hymn, a line from a play or a piece of text – with which we are very familiar and which provides us with comfort, courage and reassurance.

The familiarity of the Guide Law is far more than being able to repeat it off by heart. It is the familiarity which provides a framework for action and to which we can turn in moments of uncertainty and doubt. Yet it is also a familiarity which can challenge, inspire and excite.

**In the familiar I find the strength
to face the unknown.**

The Promise should be discussed, looked at, dissected and then put back together again. How else can we grow in our understanding and acceptance of our Promise?

My daughter was renowned for asking her Physics teacher "Why?" She needed to talk theories out and clarify her ideas. We all do this with current news items, governmental changes, and changes within the Association. We discuss them with friends, family and colleagues because we need to find out more, add to and clarify our own views, and argue with others to help us come to a clearer understanding.

So why should this not be the same for all aspects of the Promise? Without the discussion we will only have one view – ours. We need to be challenged so that our understanding will be deepened and widened.

A young Guider finishing her Warrant said to me when the Promise was mentioned, "Well I suppose this means I won't get a Warrant with my unconventional views". She did and I was challenged in my interpretation and understanding.

Yes, the Promise has to be discussed, dissected and put back together just like everything else in Guiding.

As we share in discussion and exchange ideas so our understanding grows.

Guiding is special.... To us it has become a way of life.

Guiding is special because it offers many opportunities to meet new friends and have fun.

The skills and experiences gained through Guiding influence life outside Guiding for the better.

Guiding may become a way of life but it should not overrule life. Outside interests keep ideas fresh and help to keep the meaning of Guiding in perspective.

**Being in the Guides is not just
a part-time affair for me.
It is a way of life of which I am truly proud.**

I have thought, thought and thought again about the Promise.

Thinking is essential to establish for oneself a basic understanding of the Promise, but the best way to absorb it and make it part of our life is to *live* it. Guiding is an active organisation and it is essentially by doing that we learn.

So let's roll up our sleeves and make the Promise live in our lives. Loving God by recognising His work in creation and glorying in it. Serving the Queen and helping other people by upholding her in our prayers and trying to be responsible citizens.

In keeping the Guide Law we must aim for perfection, recognise when we fall short and not be disheartened by failure, but be encouraged to try again. In the end all we can do is 'do our best'.

As a Guide I should be 'doing', not just 'aspiring'.

__The young people of today, more than ever before, need something definite to hold on to.__

In a world of uncertainty Guiding can help to meet that need. In the guidelines of the Promise and Law it affirms by implication that life has a meaning – one that, at the very least, has something to do with the quality of our relationships with:
• one another,
• the natural world of which we are part,
• the creative spirit, whom we call God, at the heart of it all.

The experiences that come through taking part, with others, in a fully balanced Eight Point Programme can't help but develop an awareness of these relationships, and the giving and receiving they involve, in daily life; through the doing comes growing understanding. There will always be more to discover and much remains a mystery, but the guidelines give something to hold on to as we explore.

The Promise is like the guideline on a blindfold trail. It is always there and is a reliable base from which to face the unknown.

Lord Baden-Powell, assisted by his sister, Agnes, laid the foundations of a worthwhile Movement for all ages. Those foundations are as relevant today as they were then, even if girls no longer 'help to build up the Empire'. The Promise and Law is at the heart of those foundations.

If foundations are strong and simple then what is built on top of them can be as fragile and complex as the architect is able to make the structure. The simplicity and strength of the Promise and Law, our foundations, allow for the flexibility and freedom which today's Guide experiences.

In the freedom to explore for herself and her community she is able to participate in challenge, fun, adventure and sharing – elements of B-P's original vision and still part of The Guide Association's vision today.

From the foundations of the Promise and Law come the foundations of life – life in relationship with others and with God.

The Promise and Law is my springboard to life's exciting journey.

We must remember that the Promise starts with "I will do my best...". All children understand that. They are five words which are crucial to the rest of the Promise and which validate all the rest.

No other person can measure "my best" but me.

I know, at the end of a task, whether I deserve the prize, the badge or the marks I have been given. These sorts of rewards may be surprisingly unimportant when it comes to it. It isn't that other people's judgements don't matter, only that I am the hardest and the fairest judge of what I do.

When I determine "to do my best", I am saying that I will:
• be tough on myself – in demanding the greatest endeavour and the greatest commitment I can muster;
• respect myself – in giving credit to my strengths and acknowledging the new efforts that will be required;
• be kind to myself – in recognising my starting point and having patience with myself as I hit the obstacles along the way.

Deep inside myself – in my soul – alongside my values and my conscience, I keep the measure of "my best".

*Once words are learned, their meaning
can deepen throughout life. If someone
does learn something by heart, that suggests
it is meaningful to them.*

As children we learn many things 'parrot-fashion' in order to recall them: there is a purpose in the initial learning.

Having learned the Promise with help and explanation, a young member will have a basic understanding of its meaning.

As we face new experiences in life so we recall our Promise and find a deeper meaning. In our relationships with family and friends and in facing difficult times in life we can use the Promise as a guide.

How often have words of hymns and prayers previously sung or said from memory suddenly been more meaningful when appropriate to our thoughts or experience at that moment?

**The real challenge is living the words,
not learning them.**

I have always understood that our Promise is central to all we do. (The Guiding Manual paragraph 1.3: "Central to what Guiding stands for... is the Promise".)

Without an acceptance of the principles contained in the Promise, there is no justification for the Guide Programme. What right has any of us to channel and direct the thinking, actions and aspirations of girls who choose to belong to our Movement without any recognition of a supreme being, the Creator and source of hope for the future, and without some understanding of our human responsibilities in relation to the future?

The open-ended and unknown aspects of the development of a girl's character, skills and abilities through her undertaking to do her best, in whatever sphere of activity and involvement the Programme may offer, are exciting!

Guiding may play only a small part in a girl's development, or it may be a major influence. Let us offer her the opportunities our Promise gives.

The young people of today, more than ever before, need something definite to hold on to.

We live in ever-changing and sometimes difficult times. Young people in many cases find confusion in their lives and little which is safe and secure. There is a danger that they will drift aimlessly around like a wind-blown leaf in a stream.

To cross safely to the other side of the stream, help is needed. Stepping stones across the turbulent water are a sure way of safely gaining the other bank with a willing hand offered to help as you cross.

The Guide Promise and Law is our stepping stone in life, safe and secure, guiding us as we go. It is worth holding on to as we help the young people of today.

**Safe stepping stones across the stream
are there forever.**

*The Law and Promise are two distinct
elements: the Law describes the sort of person
we should be and the way we should behave;
the Promise is our commitment to try to live
our whole lives like that.*

Sometimes it is said that young people nowadays don't know what is *wrong*, as society generally is less insistent on high moral standards. Our Law shows clearly and unambiguously what is *right*. The words used are simple enough for a child to understand, learn and try to keep; yet they become ever more meaningful as we grow older and relate these words to our adult lives.

Sometimes it is said that you can't join Guides if you don't believe in God. This is a misunderstanding. A girl may *join* Guides even though she may never have had the opportunity to know about God, because she cannot know if she wants to become a Guide unless she attends its meetings and events.

Our great endeavour is to show her – through the exciting activities, the wonders of nature, the kindliness of her companions, and the example of her leaders – the glory and the love of God, so that when the time comes she is ready to make her Promise with confidence.

**The Law strengthens my understanding of right
and wrong. My Promise challenges me to do right.**

Familiar words learned by heart will grow in meaning as we mature. At any level of maturity we can only promise according to our understanding and experience of those words.

Words learned by heart are never forgotten, even if their meaning is not always thought about very deeply. When we actually do stop to think about them, we may well find that our understanding of them has expanded in line with the expansion of our minds as we grow older.

This does not mean that our earlier interpretation was wrong, or somehow second-rate, for our understanding at any moment is fitting for the person we are then.

The Promise I make now is not made by the person I was last year, or will be next year; it is made by the one I am now.

The Promise is like a root of the tree, take away the root and it withers and dies.

The Promise has always been central to the Guide Movement. Keeping it has held us firm, kept us in touch with one another, and enabled us to grow as people.

When we lose something that has been central to our life, a part of ourselves is lost too; a hole is left within us that remains empty.

Like the root of a tree the Promise has been a way for so many of finding nourishment in all sorts of conditions. Firmly rooted in our being, we depend on its strength and support. We may not know how it works, but we know without doubt its effect.

Keeping in contact with the root will sustain our life, and our branches, leaves, flowers and fruit, will be formed and grow in abundance.

The Promise and Law is a living force.

It is the responsibility of each one of us to enable others, and particularly the girls, to be able to express what the Promise means to them – at their particular stage of development – and to help them to see that their understanding is not static.

We repeat our Promise at different stages in Guiding and it can mean different things as we mature, develop and are changed by experiences within our lives. We have continually to assess our behaviour, whether our Promise is challenging us enough and how we can strive to improve our understanding.

It is necessary to explain to girls that they are unique individuals and that their Promise will not necessarily mean the same thing to them as it does to their friends.

I thank God that I am unique and can bring and share my own understanding of the Promise.

Let's try and give people a pride in themselves.

Often pride is immediately jumped on as a quality which promotes self to the detriment of others, but this need not necessarily be so. Pride is a quality which needs to be worked at, it needs to be balanced with other characteristics of our personalities and aspects of life and yes, I think we should be trying to give young people a pride in themselves.

- Pride in the talents and gifts they have been given, and direction to use these in the service of others rather than seeking glory solely for themselves.

- Pride in who they are, as people journeying through life, often taking wrong turns and arriving at dead ends, but honest travellers, seeking a destination in life, and who have respect for their fellow travellers.

- Pride as young people who belong to a Movement, who have said that in the Promise and Law there is a code for living and a vision of an ideal they want to ascribe to and aim for.

Be true to yourself and you will be true to others.

The Promise is central to all our thoughts, all our activities and all our guidance of the girls who turn up to meetings week after week.

We may not think that the Promise has much to do with pitching a tent or sorting jumble. But it's there if we are there, in the fact that we care, are willing to share and enjoy the task as we do it.

It's not the great acts of worship and national service projects that demonstrate our commitment to the Promise but rather our everyday actions: we checked for litter, we asked before we used the photocopier, we waited for the others even though they are always late. (And we tried to be on time even though the others always wait!)

If we remember the Promise in small, everyday things the big special things will be a pleasure not an effort.

The Promise is with us always.

I don't care a jot if the girls can't remember it word for word; it's the ideas behind the words we want them to remember and act upon.

The Guide Promise and Law is for many of us the foundation on which we have built our understanding of trust, loyalty, courage, integrity and concern for others.

Guides need not memorise the Law, although many do, but they recognise, understand and are proud to uphold it.

For many it is a life-long commitment to the qualities that we all try to achieve. The Promise is the 'little light' we want to spread around the world.

I try to bring the Law to life in all I do.

*The Guide Promise does not say specifically that a Guide must attend a church.
Over the years, many young people and even adults, lacking standards to live by, have found them through Guiding, and have passed those standards on to their own children and others.*

Guiding is about growing – and Guiding is for all. We are all growing from different starting points, at different rates and in different ways.

We may attend a mosque, a church or a temple, or we may keep faith with our own vision of God. We may be still searching and looking for answers.

Guiding is for us all. We may have our own 'internal compass' to guide us through life or we may feel part of an uncertain world, with no values or rules.

Guiding's challenge is to welcome us all and to help us to grow, no matter where we're starting from.

We are helping young people to grow.

In an address to inspire action to promote the world-wide advancement of women, Benazir Bhutto of Pakistan, one of the great women of our time, reminded her audience of a dire prophecy by Dante: "The hottest place in Hell is reserved for those who sit on the fence in times of crisis". She was urging the men in her audience to commit themselves to the cause, saying in effect that it is no longer sufficient to sit silently on the sidelines.

In any great endeavour involving vision, energy and determination, I need to commit myself to achieve the goal. The Promise and Law represents such endeavour, and as a true Guide I should commit myself to the challenge of trying to live my life by the values that it expresses.

**Being committed to the values of the Promise
and Law means I am no longer free
for anything less.**

*Looking further into the clauses of the Law,
the more often I read them, the more I grew
to like them and understand them. In fact
I was quite excited by them.*

Each day as I go into my new garden I discover different
things. A hidden wren acclaiming loudly from the depth
of the hawthorn; glowing, glorious berries on the
rowan; snowdrops forcing their spiky leaves through the
snow, so that their nodding flowers can form a white
carpet of their own; herbs and lavender filling the air with
scents to replace that of the fading wallflowers. These I
can see, I can hear, I can smell and taste and touch. And it
is exciting!

So it is with our Guide Law. As I consider each Clause I
recall experiences from different times and places. I
question the meaning. I read and read again. I relate them
to my own life. I grow in understanding and it is exciting!

**As I grow in understanding of the Law and
accept its challenges, I discover new things and
my experience is enriched.**

For me, the Promise which I have made has given me a purpose in life and a way to follow. We are trusted to 'do our best' and who can say what each girl's best is – only the individual herself.

Our Promise is both steadfast and flexible – *steadfast* because it shines brightly at the centre of all our Guiding and Scouting; *flexible* because it is tailored to the needs and challenges of each individual Guide and Scout throughout the world.

We all promise to do 'our best' – that 'best' is different for each one of us. What is hard for me may be easy for you and vice versa. Sometimes we try to escape new responsibilities and challenges by saying that 'our best' is not good enough – that, however, is irrelevant.

No-one's 'best' should ever be unleashed against someone else's – it stands alone and is unique, as we all are.

We all know in our hearts when we have really done 'our best'.

As an adult my Guide Promise and Law has specifically proved its worth. It has a habit of popping into the mind unasked and it is of inestimable value.

As life progresses and the ups and downs are experienced, the words and implications of the Guide Law are subconsciously thought about and, whether they are heeded or not, they usually emerge to help us through difficult decision-making and hard times.

Unwrapping a Christmas parcel recently I automatically untied the string, looped it round my fingers and secured it. My family laughed and said, "Mum's at it again." They meant that I was remembering the words "A Guide is thrifty".

During a long walk in the snow it became obvious one of our party was flagging – I jollied her along with some absurdity and she laughed and said, "I know, a Guide is cheerful in all difficulties".

These trivial examples show how the Law pops into the mind unasked. Thank goodness it also comes to mind when it really matters.

**Throughout my life the Law prompts me
to do the right thing.**

> *It is a good thing to remember that we*
> *Promise 'to do our best', and no-one*
> *will be able to live up to all the standards*
> *perfectly all the time, but they are there*
> *as a shining beacon for us all to aim for*
> *in the best way we can.*

We all have days when we get out of bed on the wrong side and feel nastily out of tune with ourselves and everyone else, and days when nothing goes right and others are obstructive and awkward. At such times it is tempting to grumble, opt out and metaphorically kick the cat.

If we had no code to live by, we would have no reason to do otherwise; conversely, if we had a code that took no account of failure, we would hate ourselves for not living up to it. But a promise 'to do our best' enables us – and encourages us – to aim for what we believe to be good, whilst not despising ourselves on those occasions when we fall short.

'Doing our best' may not make us perfect,
but it brings out the best in us.

I interpret 'God' in the widest sense of the word.

Through interpreting 'God' in the widest sense of the word I am not limiting myself to a preconceived definition. I may have a personal view of God but I need to be aware of the varying beliefs of women and girls throughout the world.

It is for each of us to decide when we feel ready to identify who our God is.

Guiding is for all – whatever their beliefs.

We all fail to love our God, to practise good citizenship and to keep the precepts of the Law, but we can always – should always – succeed in continuing to 'do our best' to achieve higher standards in all these things.

Failure is a feature of life familiar to us all. We can all think of incidents and episodes that haven't worked out as we wished – failing an exam, the driving test, even failing family or friends by neglect, selfishness or thoughtlessness. We all know what it feels like to fail.

However, like the phoenix rising from the ashes, we can triumph over failure if we take time to reflect on the lessons learned from the experience. Why did this go so badly for me? How could it go better next time?

By its Method, Guiding gives us the opportunity to use failure as a means of growth; by its values, Guiding encourages us to put failure behind us and do our best to aim for its highest ideals.

The most I can do is "my best".

*It is an integral part of the rich heritage
B-P left us to enjoy, share and pass on
to future generations, and it has been
a guiding light throughout my life.*

Can I imagine Guiding without the commitment of our threefold Promise? Of course not! It would then lack that 'something extra', that sense of a shared commitment. Guiding gives the feeling of fellowship with others who have made the same Promise, wherever and whenever one meets them throughout life.

If I can help our young people to experience this spiritual bond, then this is the best gift I can give to those with whom I have the privilege of working.

**This has been my aim and objective in
my Guiding life – only others can tell
if I have achieved it.**

I interpret 'God' in the widest sense of the word since I live and work in a multi-ethnic society and Guiding is for all.

I find it very difficult to refer to God as 'She'. Maybe that is because I have never thought of God in terms of masculinity. Deity is different but doesn't have a special pronoun and 'He' seems more personal than 'It'.

Individuals must have very different perceptions of God, perceptions which depend on background and culture, on teaching and experience. If there are differing perceptions of God within one family, one church, one culture, just imagine the differences between families, between churches, between cultures.

The great thing is to remember how personal our individual perception of God is and to accept and appreciate differing perceptions in others.

As I listen to others I grow in my understanding of our infinite God.

We all need to have the opportunity to think things through.

Do you think things through? Important things such as relationships, actions, decision?

Taking time to think about them is not easy. So often we make decisions quickly because we feel we have to. Spending some time considering the possible consequences of a particular action may make the difference between going ahead and deciding against it.

Unless we make the time and seize the opportunity to stop and think, we may find ourselves regretting the decision we have made. The really important things in life are too precious to rush into heedlessly. We cannot, of course, put off indefinitely making a decision.

Sometimes after much thought we have to go ahead with our doubts still intact. We have to wait and see how things turn out. But we gave ourselves the opportunity to think it through and we are able then to live with the consequences.

Each day I take time to think quietly about some of the decisions I will have to make and try to consider their consequences.

> *As with all games, the game of Guiding has rules and playing the game means playing by those rules.*

I wonder if you have ever played croquet? A very difficult game to follow if you don't know the rules but one in which it is easy to cheat if you do! I am not comparing Guiding to croquet, or advocating cheating but it is also easier to play the game of Guiding if you do know the rules.

One has the same sense of naughtiness when avoiding keeping the Law as in cheating at croquet. I have seen that look on the face of a Guide who is thinking, "If I look as if I'm busy they may not ask me to sweep the floor at the end of the meeting" or "If I don't catch her eye she won't put the difficult new Guide in my Patrol".

She knows she is not playing the game according to the rules but she also knows that she *will* sweep the floor if she is asked and she *will* take that nuisance into her Patrol if she has to, just as the player cheerfully replaces the ball in croquet when foot movement has been spotted.

Our task is to make sure the rules are understood, not to enforce them.

**Knowing the rules of the game challenges me
to play it fairly.**

The Law seems to present a good starting place for discussions and a Programme around its meaning, which will help me to generate thoughtful debate among our members about what is expected of us as Guides.

One of my clearest memories as a Guide is of that activity when you illustrate the Clauses of the Law through mime. The cheerful grimaces through the most traumatic situations still live with me! I must confess I don't remember much discussion but presumably to produce such memorable mimes we must have talked about it first.

I *do* remember the activity and why we were doing it. This simple activity (and many others that I don't remember so clearly) have helped to make me the person I am today.

Guides 'learn by doing'; through the Programme I learn to live the values of the Law.

A true sense of belonging must be
more than just the wearing of a badge or
payment of a subscription.

A very special Guiding moment for me was when women, gathered at Sangam to celebrate its Silver Jubilee, joined together in their Guide's Own and renewed the Promise, each speaking in their own language and using their own wording of the Promise.

Over the preceding few days, life at the Centre had been frantic as the official birthday celebrations took place. Women from all over the world, most of whom had never met before, worked 'like Trojans' to ensure all went well.

The reason it *did* all work so well was because we all had one thing in common – a true sense of belonging to the world-wide Guiding family.

A sense of belonging which, in this instance, demonstrated itself in celebration, but on other occasions has given rise to acts of solidarity with women world-wide, and initiatives for peace and development. A sense of belonging which can transcend borders and boundaries, badges and subscriptions.

Guiding is a world-wide family just waiting to welcome you.

The threefold Promise is another easily understood concept – another 'rule of the game' – simple to grasp and easy to remember. A sort of shorthand to explain Guiding's aims and to show the girls the way they should be heading.

One of the Five Essentials is a commitment to a common standard. That common standard is expressed in the Promise made by every member, adult and child, to try to 'do her best' in the three dimensions of her life.

• 'To do her best to love her God'. The freedom to express God in her own terms allows for the individual to be at one with the group, everyone bringing her own culture and teaching to the kaleidoscopic understanding of the Creator.

• 'To do her best to serve her Queen and country and to help other people', recognising that we all live in a community and have responsibilities to, as well as expectations of, that community.

• 'To do her best to keep the Guide Law', making the most of herself, her opportunities, abilities and experiences.

There are three dimensions, but they relate to each other and together make a whole person.

I'll try to be true to my threefold Promise.

More people are thinking about it in a personal way as it affects them and their life.... I believe this is a good sign and shows that individuals are really searching and exploring what the Promise means for them – now.

There are those units which make constant reference to the Promise. Renewal of the Promise happens every week. Activities are related to the Promise, "Why did we do that?", "Did we think of other people when we did that?", "Let's really try and do our best in this".

By making the words live in actions each week, the girls see their relevance in everyday life and see what is different about being a Guide.

Other units often leave this side of Guiding to chance: when the opportunity occurs, when there is a Promise-making ceremony, when something of significance has happened.

Whatever the method, I feel that there is a heightened appreciation of the Promise for individuals, exploration and questioning is encouraged and we are learning that there are many different 'right' answers.

I try to make the Promise my own.

I interpret 'God' in the widest sense of the word since I live and work in a multi-ethnic society and Guiding is for all.

We all need to believe in something outside our world and our day-to-day existence. 'God', by whatever name, represents what is good in life, what is truly wonderful and what is beyond our ability to comprehend.

- 'God' means something very special to each one of us.

- 'God' is someone who is known and trusted in our hearts.

- 'God' loves us and 'God' forgives us.

- 'God' does not punish us or hurt us.

- 'God' loves us for what we are, not for what we might or should be.

As we grow, so too should our love for 'God' and our understanding about 'God's' goodness.

I will grow in my love and understanding about 'God'.

Many people are disenchanted with organised religion as they see it, but they want guidance and are seeking help. This is why many are turning to Eastern mystics.

Where are we starting our journey from? We might have a clear idea of where we are now and know where we want to go. Our compass can show us the way to choose.

Or we could be lost – in wild country, in the fog, in the dark.... Which way do we go now? We need help and guidance even to start the journey. A compass may not help us initially, if our starting point is not clear.

How we start is a very personal matter and we may find it difficult to fit our ideas into a recognised route plan.

But wherever we are starting from, our destination lies along the same road. We may need to make choices as we go; to explore, to enquire, to try to understand, but our Promise can give us the map. It can support us for some of the decisions, but still leave us with options. Those choices are ours.

**There are many different starting points
and many different routes,
but our destinations are similar.**

*More people are thinking about it
in a personal way as it affects them
and their life.... I believe this is a good sign
and shows that individuals are really
searching and exploring what the Promise
means for them – now.*

When I first made the Promise as a Brownie, the most important thing for me to do was "to do my best". This meant that I tried hard to make sure that I always did everything to the best of my ability. If I didn't, then I hadn't done the job properly and I had let myself down as I hadn't kept my Promise.

When I was a Guide, it was still important "to do my best", but also "to do my best" in helping other people. Every week I visited a lady to help her at home to make her life just a little easier. I was beginning to develop my understanding of the Promise and its relevance in my life and for the people I wanted to help.

As a Ranger I began to think about giving service not only to my local community as a Young Leader, but also to the wider world. This led me to work in a children's home in Kenya and run courses in first aid and personal development for young people in the Nairobi region.

I have grown through my greater understanding of the Promise and it has grown with me. Today I live my life through my Promise, as a code for living, always searching for the inner spirit that drives me forward to success.

Only *I* know when I have been true to my Promise.

Index

Index

Notes

Notes

Notes

Notes